Kevin and Rocky were friends.
Kevin wanted to kick the ball, but he kicked Rocky.
Rocky was cross.

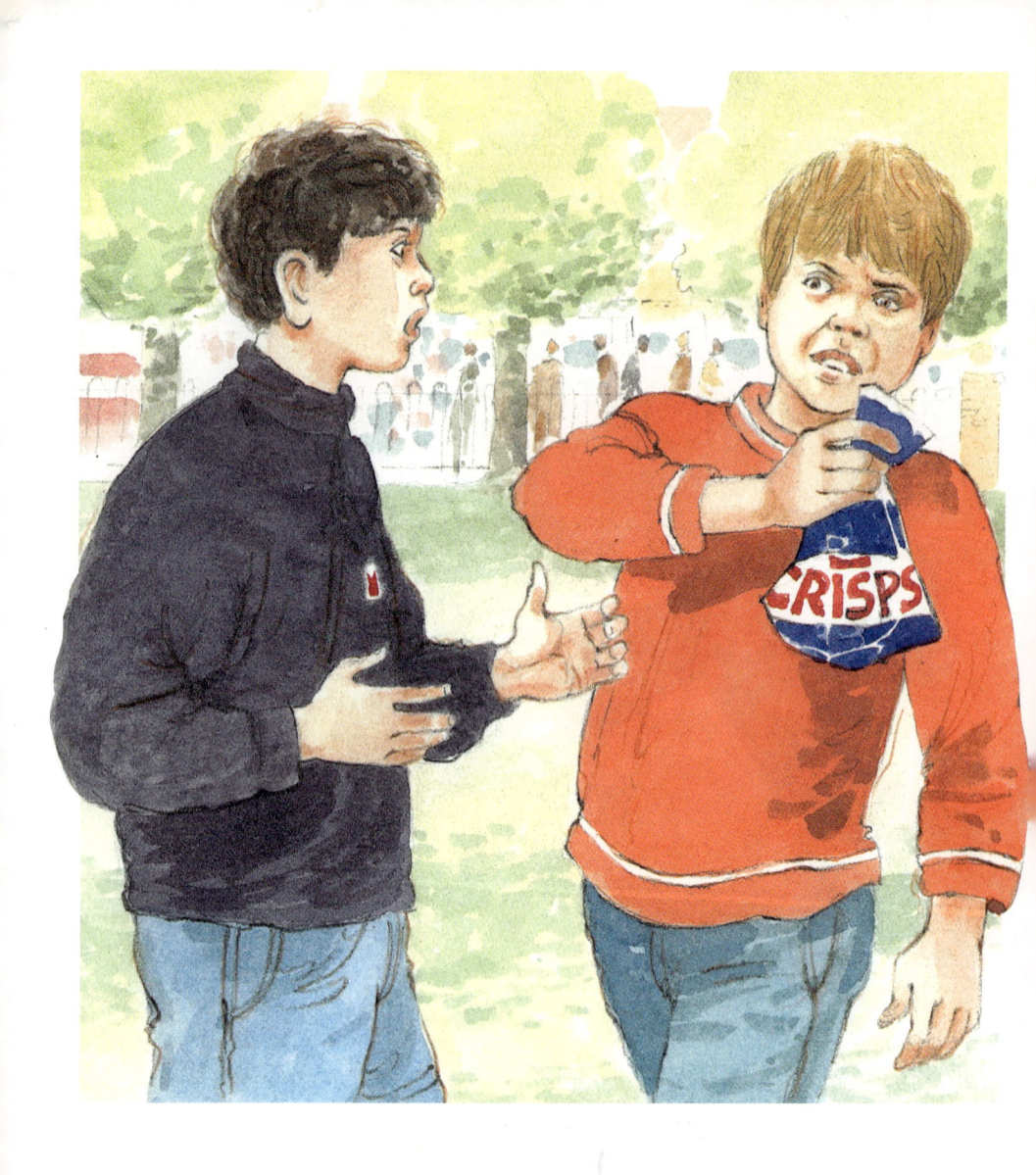

After school Kevin bought a bag of crisps.
Rocky saw Kevin and grabbed the bag.
Kevin was cross.

'My crisps!' he said. 'You grabbed my crisps!'
Mr Keeping saw Rocky and Kevin.
He was out with Bruce.

Rocky dropped the crisps all over the Square. 'See,' said Rocky, 'you have no crisps left!'

4

Kevin was cross.
He pushed Rocky.
Rocky grabbed Kevin.
Mr Keeping ran over to Rocky and Kevin.
'Let go!' he said.

The crisps were all over Kevin and Rocky.
Bruce wanted some crisps and went
over to Rocky.
'Get off, Bruce!' said Rocky, and ran away.

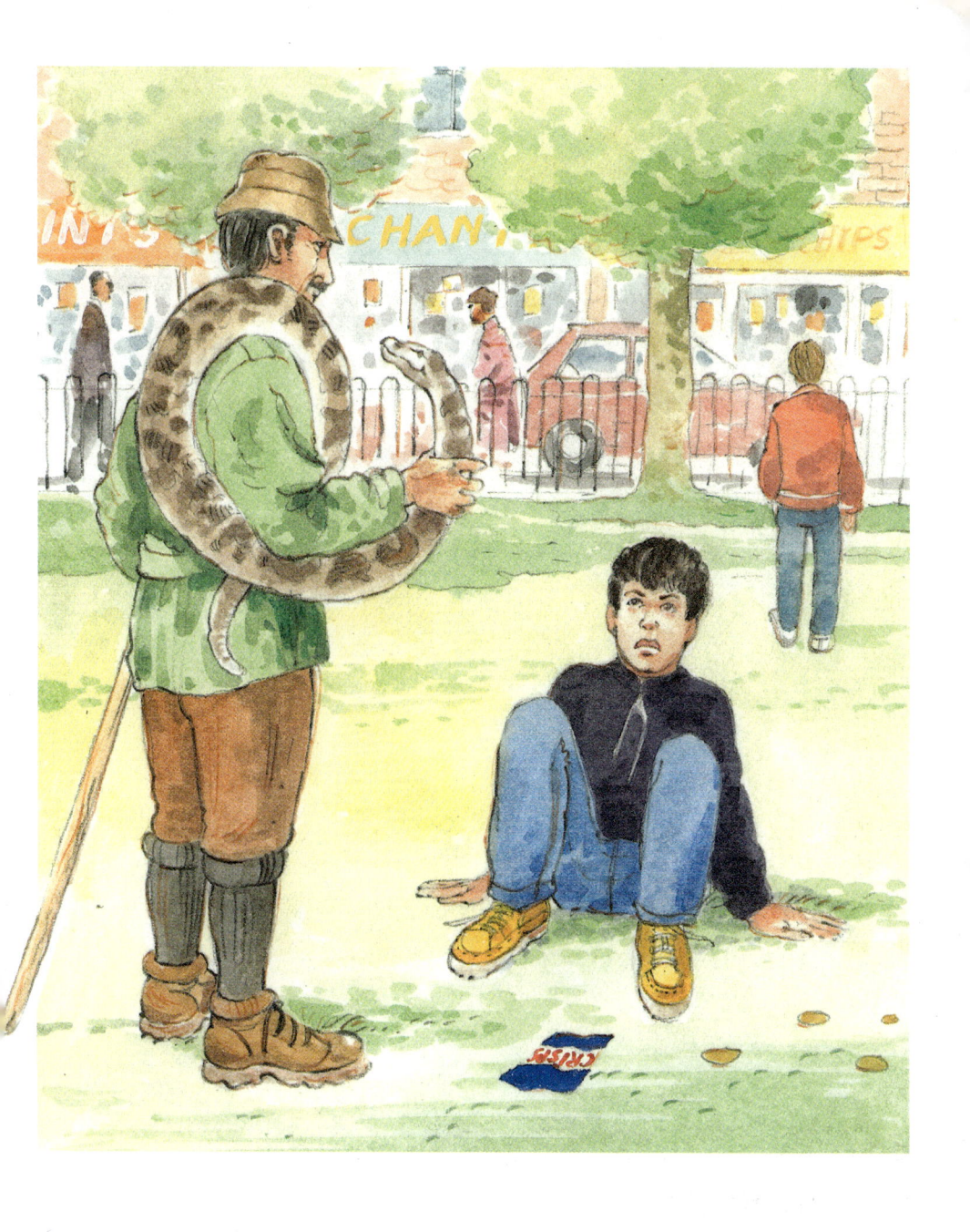

'What is going on?' said Mr Keeping.

'I wanted to kick the ball, but I kicked Rocky and he is cross,' said Kevin.

Mr Keeping went over to Rocky.
'Bruce wanted some crisps.
He was not cross with you,' said Mr Keeping.

'Kevin wanted to kick the ball.
He was not cross with you.'

Rocky was happy.
'I will go and talk to Kevin,' he said.

Rocky made friends with Kevin.
Good friends!